THE ASTOUNDING
ASTROMAZE

ROLF HEIMANN

LITTLE  HARE

The study of "astrology" (an ancient Greek word meaning "science of the stars") began thousands of years ago. The ancient Greeks used the position of the sun in the sky as a guide to the best time to plant and harvest crops. Early astrologers came to believe that the position of the stars and planets when people were born could determine their characters, and even predict future events in their lives.

Do the stars really influence our lives? There is no scientific evidence that our characters are determined by the star signs we were born under—but sometimes the accuracy of what the stars "say" can be surprising. One thing is certain, though—even if you're born under a "lucky star", you will not achieve your best without giving your best. Remember that as you navigate your way through the mazes in this book!

ARIES
Daring, adventurous
Aries wouldn't be
daunted by narrow
bridges or steep steps.
But which set of steps
will take you from
the water to the
Aries' tower?

TAURUS

Practical, reliable
Taureans love comfort,
so a bull would soon
find a path from the
wilderness to
the luxurious castle.
Can you?

GEMINI
Bright, alert Geminis
are great at overcoming
obstacles, so these
twins should have no
trouble finding a way
to each other!

CANCER
Cancerians are very loyal, and will always help a friend in need. Race to the lifesaver and rescue your friend from drowning.

LEO ☉
Proud Leos are natural leaders, and love being the center of attention. But which of these 8 starting points leads to the center stage?

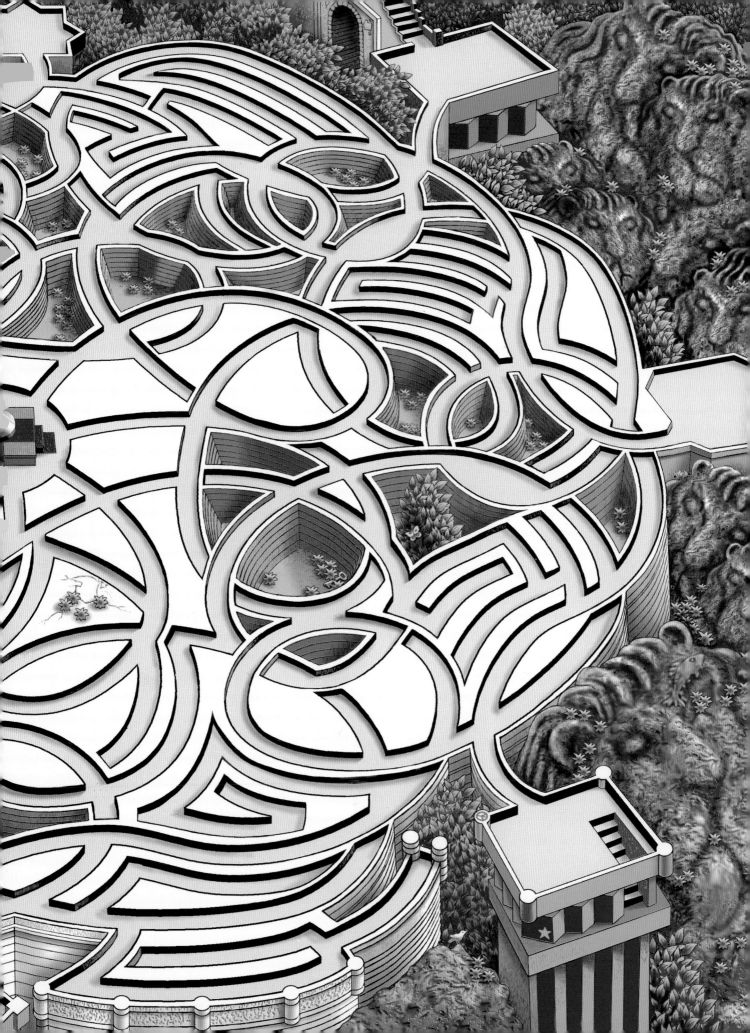

VIRGO☉
Methodical Virgos
look for the best way
from A to B. And since
they are both energetic
and patient, they
usually find it!

LİBRA
Slow and steady
Librans care and
provide for others
and always strive
for peace. Guide
the tortoise to the
peaceful resting
place at the other
side of the maze.

SCORPIO
Brave Scorpios love an exciting voyage through the unknown, but they also look forward to arriving home. This maze brings you right back where you started from.

SAGITTARIUS

Versatile Sagittarians are focused and optimistic. Focus on getting from the red target to the green one —and surely you'll do it!

CAPRICORN
Capricorns are
inventive and efficient,
but are seldom satisfied.
They are always looking
for greener pastures,
so help the goat
reach those green
hills far away.

AQUARIUS
Water carriers are very clever and responsible, so they can be trusted to water the giant pumpkin. But it's not easy to get from the well to the pumpkin!

PISCES

Musical and artistic, Pisceans love beautiful things. Can you help the spotted kingfish reach the lovely waterlily in the middle of the pond?

Nobody is perfect—as these more negative characteristics of the star signs reveal. If you don't recognize yourself in the descriptions below, remember that astrology is not an exact science. (Or maybe you are perfect after all!)

ARIES
The ram
Impatient Aries can have a very high opinion of themselves.

Born between March 21 and April 19

TAURUS
The bull
Taureans can be rather stubborn and self-indulgent.

Born between April 20 and May 20

GEMINI
The twins
Gossipy Geminis are inclined to show off.

Born between May 21 and June 20

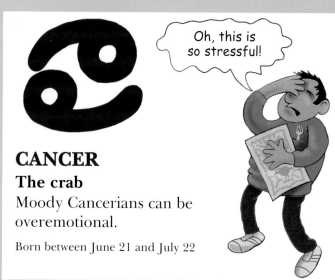

CANCER
The crab
Moody Cancerians can be overemotional.

Born between June 21 and July 22

LEO
The lion
Leos are easily embarrassed and are braggers at times.

Born between July 23 and August 22

VIRGO
The virgin
Nervous Virgos often miss the big picture.

Born between August 23 and September 22

What's your sign?

Check your birthday against the dates below to find out what your star sign is.

LIBRA
The scales
Librans can be indecisive, and are easily influenced by others.

Born between September 23 and October 22.

Maybe I should ask someone else...

SCORPIO
The scorpion
Scorpios can be spiteful and secretive.

Born between October 23 and November 22

Hey! I'm doing a maze, if you don't mind!

SAGITTARIUS
The archer
Hesitant Sagittarians can be slow to finish a task.

Born between November 23 and December 21

I'll finish it tomorrow...

CAPRICORN
The goat
Ambitious Capricorns are often dissatisfied with their own work.

Born between December 22 and January 19

I could have done better...

AQUARIUS
The water carrier
Aquarians are dreamers who tend to think too far ahead.

Born between January 20 and February 19

I'm nearly done. Then what?

PISCES
The fish
Impractical Pisceans dislike criticism.

Born between February 20 and March 20

*Well that's the way **I** do it, all right?!*

Aries

Taurus

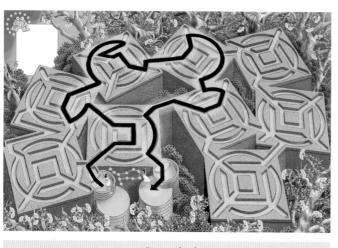

Gemini

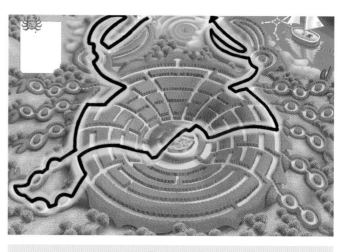

Cancer

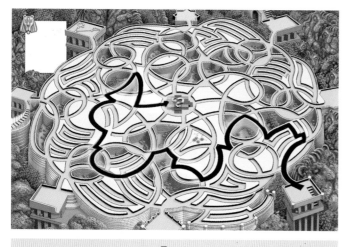

Leo

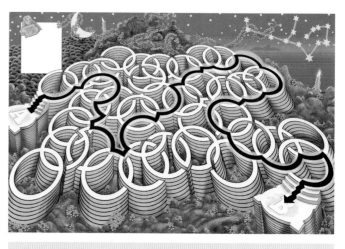

Virgo

Libra

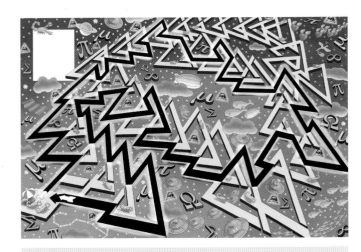

Scorpio

Sagittarius

Capricorn

Aquarius

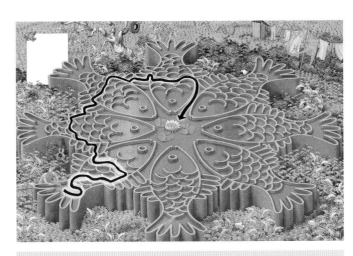

Pisces

The following things have been hidden in each maze:
A fish, a butterfly, a fork, a peace symbol , a nut , a heart,
a mushroom, a key and a mouse.
And last, but not least, Rolf has hidden an outline of Australia. He's done that in all
his pictures since he became an Australian citizen (and he never forgets Tasmania).

Little Hare Books
4/21 Mary Street, Surry Hills
NSW 2010 AUSTRALIA

First published in 2003

National Library of Australia
Cataloguing-in-Publication entry

Heimann, Rolf, 1940-.
Astromaze.

For children.
ISBN 1 877003 20 4.

1. Maze puzzles – Juvenile literature. I. Title.

793.738

Designed by ANTART
Printed in China through Phoenix Asia Pacific

5 4 3 2